STOICISM

An Ex-SPY's Guide to the Stoic Way of Life - Mindsets & Thinking Tools For Modern Day Success

JAMES DAUGHERTY

© Copyright 2018 – (James Daugherty) All rights reserved.

The contents of this book may not be reproduced, duplicated or transmitted without direct written permission from the author. Under no circumstances will any legal responsibility or blame be held against the publisher for any reparation, damages, or monetary loss due to the information herein, either directly or indirectly.

Legal Notice:

This book is copyright protected. This is only for personal use. You cannot amend, distribute, sell, use, quote or paraphrase any part or the content within this book without the consent of the author.

Disclaimer Notice:

Please note the information contained within this document is for educational and entertainment purposes only. Every attempt has been made to provide accurate, up to date and reliable complete information. No warranties of any kind are expressed or implied. Readers acknowledge that the author is not engaging in the rendering of legal, financial, medical or professional advice. The content of this book has been derived from various sources. Please consult a licensed professional before attempting any techniques outlined in this book.

By reading this document, the reader agrees that under no circumstances are is the author responsible for any losses, direct or indirect, which are incurred as a result of the use of information contained within this document, including, but not limited to, —errors, omissions, or inaccuracies.

TABLE OF CONTENTS

Introduction v

Chapter 1: Purpose Over Passion 1

Chapter 2: Persistence & Massive Action -
　　　The Magic Formula 7

Chapter 3: Do What You Say You Will -
　　　Ditch Excuses! 13

Chapter 4: Re-contextualization - Obstacles
　　　Are Gateways to Success,
　　　Not Doorways to Failure 17

Chapter 5: Goal Setting & Properly
　　　Assessing Progress 23

Chapter 6: Delaying Gratification 31

Chapter 7: The Power of Gratitude 35

Chapter 8: Use Role Models Wisely 39

Chapter 9: Die Before You Die 43

Summary 47

Conclusion 55

Bonus Chapters 57

INTRODUCTION

"How long are you going to wait before you demand the best for yourself?"

(Epictetus)

I have long been obsessed with uncovering the principles which most effectively lead to success in any undertaking in life. My own has been a testing ground for these tenets. Self-discipline, self-reliance, persistence in overcoming adversity and so on. A crucible in which these elements were mixed and refined on a near daily basis. Although I didn't know it at the time, in essence, this training lead me to becoming a professional Stoic.

I am now fascinated with this philosophy. I studied the work of Marcus Aurelius, Epictetus and Seneca in such detail, that I knew their minds as if I'd lived alongside them. My first book on the subject included many of these first principles, affirmations and meditations the forefathers of Stoicism provide us. The nuggets of wisdom which identify and clarify the inherent struggles of life, but also the virtues by which we can rise above them.

My second installment in the series took this one step further. It was an attempt to explore the emotional side of this scenario. The strategies which are critical in order to harness the power of these base Stoic principles. To begin to dig deep on some of the practical ways to integrate these teachings to best effect in your own life.

But I quickly realized this was only part of the puzzle. There was a final element one needs to add into the layer cake of psychological tools. One which deals with tangible success seeking behaviour, not simple adversity training and emotional regulation. But rather a proactive playbook for progress. This third book is therefore the icing on the cake in terms of mindset training. The day-to-day thinking patterns required to ensure you act in the most beneficial ways for you. To ensure you operate in a manner which best suits your interests. To get ahead of potential troubles, but also tapered to the modern day world we live in.

This is not a selfish endeavor by any means. You have to begin by fixing your own mindset before you can work on others. If you can successfully do this, you will find the relationships you have will naturally improve as a result. You will be the positive example for others to follow. They will gravitate towards you and emulate your behaviors. "Waste no more time arguing what a good man should be. Be One." As Marcus Aurelius so eloquently points out.

If you've happened to have read either of those previous books in this series, then you know who I am by now, and where I've come from. If you haven't, lets just say I have experienced a rather unique and testing set of circumstances over the years. Trials

STOICISM

and tribulations as an American FBI agent, and later on as a CIA intelligence operative.

I'll save you the details on that again here though. For now, I want to get straight into the final year material, so you can graduate from the hard knocks school of Stoicism. To outline the principles which can smooth your trajectory to a harmonious and successful life, even propel you there at record speed if you make the conscious effort to implement them without delay. So with that said, lets waste no further time and dive in.

CHAPTER 1: PURPOSE OVER PASSION

"It's time you realized that you have something in you more powerful and miraculous than the things that affect you and make you dance like a puppet."

(Marcus Aurelius)

If you wish to fix your mindset in the proper fashion, then you have to start at the top. From where it all begins regarding why any of us do what we do. This involves the high level reasoning which guides our daily actions and ensures the subsequent psychological principles fall into place more easily. There is currently some debate over what this should be for people I.e. your purpose or your passion?

These may seem synonymous with one another and could be argued that we are simply debating semantics here. Although there are a few subtle yet distinct nuances which can make all of the difference. Passion is typically self-centered, purpose usually requires contribution. Nobody can convince me that the highest form of human happiness and sense of fulfillment, does not come from eventually helping others along the way. Building steadfast relationships with family, friends and your community at large. It's the tip of Maslow's pyramid and hierarchy of needs in terms of self-actualization.

Purpose often entails doing things you do not necessarily want to do, but often times the things which are most important for your development and personal growth. If that requires getting up in front of a group of people to give a speech, then so be it. A fear of public speaking will just have to be gotten over. I can assure you its far easier to speak in front of crowds when you believe in the message you are giving. When you are delivering your purpose to the world.

"When you are finding it hard to wake up early in the morning, think this: 'I am getting up to do a human being's work. Do I still resent getting up if I am going out to do that which I was born for and brought into this world? Or was I framed for this, to keep myself warm by lying under the bedclothes?"

(Marcus Aurelius)

This passage from Marcus Aurelius' *Meditations* reminds us of the importance of doing our duty and fulfilling our responsibilities. Apart from our personal and professional requirements, we also have a duty to others, in order to build a better society and civilization in general. This is why one of the basic Stoic principles is Philanthropy, the virtue and action of giving back, not simply acquiring for oneself.

STOICISM

Passion on the other hand is more individualistic. It pertains much more to personal tastes and wants. It suggests that you should only be doing what you like to do. I find this advice shallow at best. I really dislike the notion of simply "doing what you love". In reality, we just don't live in an age where this is viable yet. Yes there maybe some future wealth and resource utopia where nothing needs to be done apart from ones own making. A place where days can be filled with basket weaving and scuba diving if we so wish.

However, I still believe this wouldn't satisfy our dominant human desire to grow ourselves, which almost always comes as a results of helping others to grow. It requires leadership and responsibility. I'm also of the opinion that you are likely to corrupt your passion if you attempt to make a career from it. If you strive to monetize your passion then you will almost certainly taint it in some way with the need to make it commercially viable or meet some productivity deadline of others. It waters down your work in a way which is unacceptable to most people.

We are guilty of looking at the few stand outs in society who have indeed managed to make it big doing what they love. However, these folks are few and far between. They are the Micheal Jackson's of music or Michael Jordan's of sport. But when you look more closely, these guys always have both the raw physical attributes along with the obsessive drive to achieve massive success in their field, but without compromising their work. If you have the ability to become a professional musician or athlete, then by all means do it. I'm not about crushing anyone's dreams here. But the reality is that for every person who attains a record deal or contract in the NBA, there 10,000 who fail trying.

If there is a market for your passion and your abilities meet the requirements to be world class, then go for it. But better advice to the vast majority of people is to find something you are competent at. Something you don't dislike entirely and there are other people, preferably mentors, who you can learn from until you can contribute yourself. You are then free to practice your passion or hobby and express yourself without being hamstrung by financial burden.

It's finally important to point out that finding your purpose is no easy task. It's not like sitting in a dark room and meditating until it comes to you. Yes it will eventually be served up by your subconscious mind during one of the quieter moments. Whilst driving or in the shower for instance. But it will take much work and deliberation first. It may take several years or even decades of trying things, jobs, activities, career paths and so forth. Some people will find it relatively early on in their 20's. Others during mid-life in their 40's. Heck some folks won't even find it until they retire!

What really matters is actively looking for it. Doing the physical and cognitive work to identify exactly what your purpose is. Most people will try a few business models or activities and become dejected when they fail to make a success of them. Or they do not produce the results they are looking for immediately. They get mentally "beat up" and give up searching for their true purpose. What they fail to realize is that all of this trial and error is part of the process of growing, as well as weeding out all of the things you don't like!

In my opinion life isn't a journey, its a process. One which needs to be navigated correctly at each level. To be experienced fully before moving onto the next stage. Think of it like completing a level of a computer game. It often requires defeating some boss villain or complex task in order to progress, each more difficult than the last. Life is no different. You have to get through mental roadblocks and moments of uncertainty in order to grow, transcend your current level, and ultimately find your true calling.

But that's the game, that's the process, and it's performed successfully via focus and persistent action. If you are unsure of what this truly requires, then the following chapter will show you the blueprint on exactly what you need to be doing.

CHAPTER 2: PERSISTENCE & MASSIVE ACTION - THE MAGIC FORMULA

"Progress is not achieved by luck or accident, but by working on yourself daily"

(Epictetus)

So now that you know its actually purpose we need to focus on, its time to go to work. If you have already found what this purpose is, or have a good idea of the direction you need to be heading, then in truth it won't feel like work. It will simply be doing what you were put on this planet to do I.e. to actualize and manifest these goals into the physical reality.

Again, this doesn't come from mere contemplation alone. It takes action, a lot of action. This is where most people trip themselves up. They get a momentary spurt of motivation, but give up on a new venture or activity at the first or second sign of trouble. We will talk in greater depth regarding obstacles and re-contextualization later on. However, for now its suffice to say that the magic comes from persisting past these set-backs. It lies on the other side of these hurdles.

Oil companies don't make money by drilling shallow hole after shallow hole. They do their research and calculations and drill a well deep enough until they hit the oil deposits. Those who benefited most handsomely from the mid-west gold rush did so by drilling until they eventually hit the vein they were aiming for, not stopping "3 feet from gold". It's as through our existence on this earth has been set up solely to test the will of human beings. To reward those with the persistence to push through problems.

In essence, you have to be a dolphin. Look around, make a plan, and be decisive about the direction you want to go in. Then dive and swim and swim and swim for 6 months before eventually surfacing for air to re-evaluate things. Then after some adjustments dive and plough again! I appreciate this is easier said then done in today's fast moving world with untold amounts of distractions. But you will be amazed at how much you will be able to achieve by sticking to this simple productivity principle.

It's funny because this book and series in general was largely written to aid people in thinking more clearly in order to lead more successful, fulfilling and ultimately peaceful lives. Although one thing I have found to help out dramatically in this regard is this notion of constant action. When you are working toward your goals 24/7 you don't have time for negative thought patterns.

STOICISM

You also now genuinely believe you deserve the success you are generating, which in turn allows you to create even more. It becomes a self-fulfilling prophecy of positive results. You start to work even harder to the point it doesn't feel like work anymore, just sweet tasting success. How good would that be! Working on things in line with your bigger picture purpose whilst creating the results of your dreams.

Ultimately you get from life what you deserve, not what you desire. Of course we all start from different vantage points regarding socioeconomic conditions and geographical factors. However it's what you make of these circumstance which matters. As the saying goes "If you are born poor, that is not your fault. But if you die poor that's on you." I don't want this to get political but you get the point. You honestly know how hard you have worked. If you have busted your tail, then you will be highly unlikely to self-sabotage those efforts when it does come time to reap the rewards.

I'm not talking about neglecting ones thoughts or sweeping things under the carpet so to speak. Its clear from my previous advice and stoic teachings in general, that facing problems head on is the best way to go. But consistent massive action allows you to push right past most of the petty things which hold us back each day. They just cease to be problems anymore.

It's said that a man is judged by the size of the things which bother him. I couldn't agree more with this. Save your problem solving energy for the big things, the real problems and curve balls which will inevitably come your way. For the things which you can seldom plan for anyway. Think of the times you had a family member fall ill, or was in a car crash. You just dealt with it at the time and got through it just fine. You had no other choice!

> "Never let the future disturb you. You will meet it, if you have to, with the same weapons of reason which today arm you against the present"
>
> (Marcus Aurelius)

So just get on with ploughing for your goals without distractions and you'll be just fine. We do need to make the distinction between being busy and being productive though. It's pointless to fill up your day with activity for activities sake. You need to work both hard and smart. You've heard the saying that "If you want something done, then give it to a busy person." I would argue you should give the task to the productive person. This is because these people are conditioned to get results, not just fit a lot into their day. They have trained themselves to achieve a certain amount of output, so adding just one more activity is of little disruption.

STOICISM

But these people weren't always this way. Everyone has this innate drive and persistent hunger as kids. It's not until we see the rest of society making excuses and allowances for why things aren't working out, and justifications for throwing in the towel. It takes a mental switch and much practice on a daily basis to become a high performing person once again. I get more done in a day then anyone I know. But I still feel lazy and bogged down at least 2-3 times a day. It takes a conscious effort to recognize these instances and to reaffirm my purpose in order to snap back into the correct state for action.

Once you do this trick enough times your identity begins to change from a person who gets moderate amounts of stuff done, to getting everything and anything done at once! You simply need to increase your activity thermostat. It helps to be around other high performance people. It's often said that you are the aggregate of the five people you most commonly associate with. Or "show me your friends, and I'll show you your future".

This is just a natural law. We all acclimatize to the environment we find ourselves in. If the guy next to you is making 5 sales a day and you are making 10, you are killing it right? But what if you moved desks next week and were positioned next to the guy doing 20 sales per day? Now the environment has changed along with your outlook. Now you feel like the underachiever, not the superstar.

This is when your action taking and persistence goes to new levels. Always be aware of your surroundings and audit them often. For 99% of people, it will need to be upgraded in order to achieve the higher goals, purpose and potential you are capable of.

CHAPTER 3: DO WHAT YOU SAY YOU WILL - DITCH EXCUSES!

"Although this has happened to me, it is my good luck that I can bear it without becoming distressed, neither being beaten by the present nor afraid of the future".

(Marcus Aurelius)

Now that we know we are striving towards our ultimate purpose, which requires constant action and persistent work. It's time to add another layer. To include another psychological string to your bow in order to ensure you can counteract bad habits and lack of motivation when they do arise. This involves always doing what you say you will do. Not only to others, but most importantly to yourself.

I always find it interesting how most people will show up on time for arrangement's with others. They will turn up 15 minutes early for a dentist appointment or business meeting, but 15 minutes late for a workout or mediation session they have scheduled for themselves. I'm certainly not suggesting you begin wasting other peoples time, simply start respecting your own to the same degree.

Doing this will ensure that you take maximum responsibility for yourself and your actions. Nobody is going to take care of your own success in life for you. Whether that be in business, academia or within the family setting. All of these areas require work which only you can do. Military personnel will have an advantage here, as they are all too aware of the importance of self-sufficiency and extreme ownership of responsibility.

Excuses will just not cut it when you are being berated for not getting your team across the assault course line in time, heaven forbid you didn't make your bed properly that morning. You learn that excuses aren't relevant anymore, results are the only thing which matters. Yes there will be reasons why something happened or didn't go your way. You were over looked for that promotion because your boss prefers your colleague he also plays golf with. You got turned down for that date because you weren't smart enough or good looking enough.

If you allow these things to dictate why something did or did not happen to you, then you surrender your power to fix them. That is really the crux of the matter. Become so invaluable that your boss has no choice but to promote you. Become so eligible that every girl or guy in your town is knocking down your door to date you.

It's not denying reality or beating yourself up for no reason. It's a mindset which is simply the most beneficial for you to adopt.

STOICISM

If everything is your fault and your responsibility to fix, then the ultimate power lies with you. You become the driving force in your own life and circumstances. In essence you now have complete control over your future and can steer the ship in the right direction.

"Fate leads the willing, and drags along the reluctant"

(Seneca)

It's my opinion that every major psychological growth spurt in life is preceded by a definite and conscious choice to assume more responsibility. It might be taking that promotion which requires handling more staff, having a child or up-sizing your home. Each of these instances takes an upgrade in the cognitive work you must perform to ensure you can handle the responsibility, and adequately deal with an expansion of your comfort zone. However, when you are fully committed to persistent and massive action towards your true purpose, your creative faculties will be purring along nicely. You will find a way around any problem as your desire is big enough to solve it. If your "why" is big enough, you'll figure out the "how to".

Progress in life will always cause additional and bigger problems to fall of your plate. Its the surest sign you are heading on the right path to growth. Don't make things anymore difficult for yourself by leaning on excuses for why you can't get past these roadblocks. I do not see issues as potential points of failure, but rather sign posts to success. It simply requires a small adjustment in your thinking. One which is well worth making, one which is described in greater detail in the following chapter.

CHAPTER 4:
RE-CONTEXTUALIZATION - OBSTACLES ARE GATEWAYS TO SUCCESS, NOT DOORWAYS TO FAILURE

"How does it help…to make troubles heavier by bemoaning them?"

(Seneca)

Everybody has heard the popular NLP phrase "The map in not the territory" regarding the true nature of reality. It suggests that things are not set in stone within our physical existence. But rather it is perception, or more accurately, projection which is the biggest determining factor in the materialistic world. Ultimately what is true for you, is true. Quantum mechanics has been pointing this out for almost a century now.

Observations such as the double slit experiment illustrate that atoms (which make up all material things) are not solid structures at there base levels. They are vibrating particles which exist in quantum "superpositions" whose wave functions do not collapse until a conscious being observes them. Crazy stuff right.

However, you do not need to fully understand these concepts in order to improve your own standing in life. We can simply play at the more superficial level within our own minds. Which pertains to fully grasping the notion of re-contextualization of our ideas, especially regarding the important junctures such as thoughts of failure and success.

It's perhaps best to give you an idea of what I mean here to begin with. If I were to make the statement that "A man is jumping". What is the first image which comes to mind? You likely envisaged some guy jumping up and down in the street or maybe in some sporting context like playing basketball. What if I then inserted "A man is jumping on a trampoline". Now your image has changed. Another layer of information has been added to the picture.

What about "A man is jumping on a dead cat or jumping in front of a car to save a small child". Once again the image is altered radically. How about "A man is jumping to conclusions or down his wife's throat". Again a completely different re-contextualization of the statement which can essentially go on forever!

So how can we utilize this concept to serve us better in everyday life? One of the most important areas to do this in my opinion, is with the set-backs and obstacles we face. We have contextualized problems as bad or negative, when in fact we should be doing the opposite. We should go looking for problems! As I previous mentioned, they are the only way you can grow and achieve success. Results are literally lying on the other side of an unsolved issue. It's these things others aren't willing to do which will set you apart, and the bigger the obstacle you can surmount, the more profound the payoff will be!

It's the very definition of being an entrepreneur, a self-starter or problem solver. It's about connecting the dots in product creation, marketing strategies or logistics and supply chain improvements in efficiency. Even if you are working within a company, it's critical for employees, management and certainly directors to do this on a daily basis. Do what others aren't willing to do and you'll get what others aren't able to get. It does require thinking though, which is the problem for most people. Henry Ford once stated that "Thinking is the hardest work there is, that's why so few people do it". I couldn't agree more.

We also associate problem solving with some degree of risk too. We are conditioned to believe that risk is inherently bad. However you aren't going to get around obstacles without sticking your neck on the line in some way. I'm not suggesting to fly into situations with reckless abandon. You need to do as much strategizing and preparation as possible before implementing your plan to move forward. But at some point you have to enter that uncomfortable space of taking action.

You may fail on the first attempt, and even the second and third. But the key is to learn from these experiences, re-group, fix your strategy and go again. Note the re-contextualization in thinking which Thomas Edison demonstrated to the world when asked how he pushed through ten thousand failures when inventing the incandescent light bulb. He simply replied "I didn't fail ten thousand times, I successfully found ten thousand ways it wouldn't work".

If you combine this method of thinking with the advice from chapters 2 & 3 I.e. embody extreme action and persistence, as well as not making any excuses. Then eventually you'll be just fine. You may pick up a few bumps and bruises along the way, but that's essential to the process. You will likely find that you will begin blasting through these obstacles and barriers and onto greater tasks, just better armed then you were before!

Winston Churchill described success as "Going from one defeat to another, without the loss of enthusiasm". This is typically very difficult for the average person to do without re-contextualizing what these momentary defeats or failures mean to them in their minds. As I previously stated, they are simply the gatekeepers to growth and greater success. However, we are conditioned from very early age, to believe that mistakes are bad.

When we suffer a perceived loss we get a reduction in the "feel good" hormone serotonin. In addition to this the body releases a cascade of stress hormones including cortisol. The reverse of this occurs when we achieve small wins. An abundance of serotonin floods the system and both our emotional state and confidence levels rise considerably. This is why it's good to get on a winning streak when you can. To set small milestones to aim at and check them off each day, week and month. It's a clever cognitive trick to ensure the consistent maintenance of an emotionally positive state. More on this in the following chapter regarding goal setting and properly assessing progress.

In truth, all of these concepts will require some form of re-contextualization in your mind. But for now, the most important one to consider is with regards to set-backs and obstacles. This is due to them being the dominant factor in why people give up on their progress of striving towards their true purpose. It is possible to "flip the switch" so to speak, in order to get that same biochemical response to obstacles as you do for success.

It just takes a thought pattern interrupt in your mind when these issues show up. They should be a light bulb which switches on in your head signifying that you have found another gateway to progress. These should be exciting moments as you know that growth is just around the corner. Relish these moments, embrace them, and you'll find that you will be moving ahead at speeds you never imagined possible.

CHAPTER 5: GOAL SETTING & PROPERLY ASSESSING PROGRESS

"A man's worth is no greater than the worth of his ambitions"

(Marcus Aurelius)

Along with not viewing set-backs and obstacles in the right way. One of the biggest mistakes I also see people make when striving for success in any area of life, is with regards to goal setting. But also subsequently assessing the progress they are making when on the path to achieving them. Again, it simply requires a subtle shift in ones thinking. But one which can have a huge impact when extrapolated out over time.

Lets begin with goal setting. So many guru's and teachers get this wrong in my opinion from the self-help oriented books and material I've read. They often state that goals should be extremely specific in terms of what a person desires I.e. certain make/model of car, particular corporate position or specific dollar amount of money. But also in exactly what time-frame or date they wish to achieve it by I.e. in 6 months or by such and such a date.

Whilst I agree with this thinking to some degree, especially with regards to shorter term goals. I believe its bad advice for the bigger things though, the longer term goals folks want to achieve. Here's why. The human brain simply does not work in this way. The subconscious mind, which is ultimately responsible for serving up opportunities to realize these bigger targets, does not work in specifics. It works in images, feelings and emotions.

In my experience its far better to split goal setting up into two main categorizes. Lets begin with the first set, the short term goals:

Short Term Goals (1-6 months)

"If a man knows not which port he sails, no wind is favorable."

(Seneca)

This is where I believe its OK to be super specific. These are the tangible KPI style metrics you may encounter in a sales job for instance. You may have to hit certain numbers each day, week or month. This is fine with me, as you do need short term targets to aim for to ensure maximum productivity. But also as a way to gauge short term progress. Similar to the dolphin analogy I mentioned previously, you should be setting up these target parameters before ploughing for 3-6 months and checking them off as you go.

These goals can and should be both quantifiable and time specific. They serve the purpose of appraising short term progress and allowing you to achieve those small wins which are so important for consistent serotonin & dopamine release. However, this is where short term targets end in there effectiveness.

Longer Term Goals (5-10 years)

"What man actually needs is not a tensionless state, but rather the striving and struggling for some goal worthy of him."

(Viktor Frankl)

As I have already eluded to, when you are concerning yourself with personal development, you have to really understand how the human mind works. This is especially true when dealing with longer time horizons. Larger and loftier life goals should be exactly that, a horizon which you are aiming for, but one which can't absolutely be achieved as its a hypothetical point. That's fine though as these are the purpose driven goals, the ideals you are striving for which are also constantly changing as you grow and develop. These aspirations will includes things like "becoming extremely wealthy" or "becoming a leader in business" or "having a large and wonderful family".

It's very difficult to quantify these things exactly. Exactly how much money constitutes being "extremely wealthy"? What position do you hold in what company? Exactly how many children, grandchildren are you going to have? The mind works with images and emotions regarding these instances. A far better strategy for longer term goals is to create a picture or movie in your mind about what these things would look like. How do you look and feel once you have achieved these things? What are you wearing? How are you carrying yourself?

The mind cannot differentiate between past, present and future events with regards to imagery in the mind. If you attached enough emotional context and feeling to what you are playing in your minds eye I.e. a past memory or projected future event, the body elicits exactly the same biochemical response, as if that experience was happening in the here and now. It's another NLP trick which can force the mind into believing that you have already achieved these things. Then the subconscious will go to work in order to serve up opportunities to bring them into your physical reality. Of course you have to take massive and persistent action when it does!

Another reason you shouldn't be putting exact figures and time-frames on these larger goals, is again due to limitations of the human brain. The conscious mind and rational cortexes function great as a problem solving tool, but it's essentially set-up to think in linear terms. It views progress as steady state increase in terms of some fixed percentage I.e. 50% per year. However, in reality things do not play out like this in the real world with regards to progress and success.

Studies clearly show that humans are terrible at assessing future development curves. We typically overestimate what can be achieved in 1-2 years. But significantly underestimate what we can achieve in ten years. We presume the linear progress will continue

STOICISM

in a straight diagonal line from bottom left to top right on a chart. In reality, the line of progress typically starts below our initial expectations for the first 2-3 years. Businesses take more time and work to get off the ground than we initially anticipated. But if we persist through this point, the magic starts to happen. At around the 5 year mark, things start to take off exponentially in a logarithmic type fashion. Opportunities come in at an ever increasing rate. This compounding effect means we typically end up way higher on the progress chart compared with our initial linear predictions. We are often off by a factor of 10-100 times!

As Seneca states, "The wise man is concerned only with the purpose of his actions, not their outcomes; beginnings are within our power, but the outcome is ultimately up to fortune".

This is again why we shouldn't be putting specifics on these types of goals. We are almost certainly undercutting ourselves when we do so. All of this stuff is way off your radar screens for now. No one is smart enough to accurately predict where they'll be in 5-10 years time, especially in today's world where change is occurring quicker than at anytime in human history. It's like trying to predict the weather. You can make reasonably accurate predictions from a few hours up to a few days out I.e. shorter term goals. But anything beyond this becomes an educated guess at best.

What tends to happen with these larger goals is that they change or pivot after a number of years. You might see yourself becoming a managing director of your company. But after five years you decide to start a company of your own, and end up being a super successful CEO. I have also seen it work in the reverse to this. A friend of mine wanted to own his own golf course after playing professionally for a number of years. Although after managing one course when he retired from playing, he got offered the job to oversee every PGA standard course in the US. This turned out to be triple the excitement and money he would have received from owning just one course of his own.

These things will also typically come into your life when its the right time for you. Stating that you want to be CEO in 8 years might be a horrible time for you to actualize this. It might be too early or too late in your development. This is why you shouldn't put time limits on these bigger goals. If you focus on the mental image of achieving them frequently enough, and then put in the consistent and required work on a daily basis, they will show up in your reality when its the perfect time for you!

How to Properly Assess Progress

The other mistake I often see people make when striving towards their goals and ultimate fulfillment of their potential, is not properly assessing the progress they are making. There is a very simple trick which every successful person on the planet employees when observing the path they are currently on, which is the reverse of every unhappy and unsuccessful person. That is they look back at "A" and not forward to "C".

It's a subtle yet profound correction to make. If you are someway down the track to achieving a goal you have set out for yourself, we'll call this point "B". By far the best thing you can do is turn back for a second and look at where you started I.e. point "A". Recognize how far you have come! This will fill you with a sense of achievement, and again ensuring more serotonin release spurring you onto even greater progress.

But virtually everyone struggling in life does the opposite, they look forward to point "C" and become depressed at how far they have yet to travel. It creates a cognitive dissonance in the mind which causes frustration and stress hormone release, hindering further progress from occurring. It's the difference between cycling uphill with a 50 pound backpack towards your goals or free wheeling downhill with the aid of a motorized engine.

Remember that the loftier long term goals are typically horizon goals anyway. They are constantly rolling back on you as you grow and progress. They tend to become larger and more ambitious as you go. Yes that may mean you never quite achieve them entirely, but you will be in a much better position then you would have been simply aiming for smaller goals, ones which can be checked off so easily.

It's often remarked that mans biggest tragedy in life is not setting ambitious goals and failing to attain them, but rather setting modest goals and actually achieving them. "Shoot for the stars and you'll probably hit the moon" as they say. But that's better then never leaving earths orbit. So don't short change yourself by thinking small. Instead think big with your purpose goals. It takes the same amount of effort and energy, just with tens times the payoff.

And finally, don't forget to adjust your vantage point when assessing your progress too. Turn the camera around to look back at where you've come from once in a while. It's far more rewarding and motivating then constantly staring out into the abyss of space I promise you!

CHAPTER 6: DELAYING GRATIFICATION

Much of what Stoicism teaches is to live by core values and to be guided by these virtues on a daily basis. One of the most important of these concepts is that of delaying gratification. We've all heard that "patience is a virtue". Some would argue this is innate within us and cannot be changed. As we will see shortly regarding the Stanford Marshmallow experiment, this genetic component to inherent self-discipline is certainly a factor predetermined from birth to some degree. Although like every virtue the Stoic forefathers provide us, these tendencies can, and should be cultivated within us to ultimately lead the most fulfilling life possible.

So what are we referring to specifically here? Gratification simply relates to a reward or satisfaction a person receives, typically in return for some kind of work or effort on their part. It is much healthier for us and our mindset when this effort exchange takes place before any gratification is given, and the longer you can stretch this time period between payoff and reward, the better.

We all crave gratification in some form in order to feel compensated for the value we provide. But for the benefit of our overall mental state, it's important to delay receiving rewards for the most part. Most of us readily settle for whatever comes our way and think of it as justification for what we do. Evolution has hardwired this into us over the centuries, thus making it one of the most difficult tendencies to override. We were required to eat the food we had gathered immediately and procreate today as tomorrow was never promised.

However, this is not the correct way to go about things in the 21st century, and can be really self-sabotaging in the long run. The idea is this; by foregoing some smaller and more immediate short term rewards, you will reap much bigger and better ones at some point in the future. Entrepreneurs will allude to the fact that they will go years without the luxuries most people can't give up, in order to acquire things later down the line that most people can only dream of. Think back to that initial 1-2 year period in the development curve. It's slow and painful to begin with. But continue persisting and doing things in the right manner, and the payoff soon becomes exponential.

People typically find that their mental and emotional state improves immensely when they learn to think in this way. They aren't stupid and intuitively know when they are receiving something for nothing, when they really deserve something or not. Remember we get what we deserve, not what we desire. There is much less self-sabotaging behavior or guilt when you do start to shift your thinking in this way. You know when you have done the necessary work, and you are much more likely to accept the fruits of your labor when its time to do so!

STOICISM

Stanford Marshmallow Experiment

You have almost certainly heard of this study at some point in your life, as it is equally interesting as it is revealing. The Stanford marshmallow experiment was performed in the late 1960's to early 1970's by psychologist Walter Mischel, who was a professor at Stanford University at the time.

The basic premise of these experiments was simple. To test what would happen when a set of children were given the option of accepting a small reward immediately (1 marshmallow) or a larger reward (2 marshmallows) if they could wait a short period of time. This was around 15 minutes when the tester would exit the room leaving the child alone to ponder the small reward in front of them.

The experiment is a basic test of self-control and can illustrate much about a child's mentality and potential. The researchers found that a number of participants eat the initial small reward right away; some waited a few minutes before eating it, while others waited out the entire 15 minutes in order to receive the additional marshmallow.

The most interesting findings about the study were the follow-up research tests which were conducted on the same child participants during their high school years, then later in adult life. The researchers found that in almost every case, the children who could wait it out for the larger reward I.e. to delay gratification, had better life outcomes when measured for everything from SAT scores, academic achievement, body mass index and a host of other markers for quality of life.

It's fairly safe to say that either naturally having a self-disciplined approach to rewards or intentionally cultivating such a mindset is beneficial for us in so many ways. Like every concept I am suggesting in this book, it simply takes a small but subtle change in your outlook towards them. If you want to build a skyscraper, you do it by perfectly laying one brick at a time. As always, take the proper and required action in a persistent manner, and you'll be just fine. Learn to love and trust the process, and the rewards will take care of themselves.

CHAPTER 7: THE POWER OF GRATITUDE

Stoicism in a nutshell is simply a playbook for dealing with adversity. Much of life is hardship and suffering, so dealing with these times adequately in a virtuous manner is a noble aim to strive for. The thinking tools I have laid out within these chapters are designed to help you do just that. To train your mind to habitually think more successfully in order to deal with any set-backs more efficiently. This ensures that any problems you do face have much less impact on you. One of the best ways of doing this is to cultivate an "attitude of gratitude" so to speak.

To be genuinely thankful for the good times, the moments of joy we all experience throughout our day, no matter how large or small. To stay humble, remain a student and be thankful for what you do have. This honestly changed my life when I made this small switch in my mind. I used to believe that being grateful for the sake of it was silly. I viewed it as a weak mentality. Why should I be thankful for these small & menial things in my life? My day was filled with much more dangerous and complex situations. Add to the fact that I had much larger goals for myself in general.

But the mind doesn't work this way. The subconscious aims to serve you more of what you are felling right now. If you are abundantly happy and grateful for what is in your present existence, then it will go to work on finding other such situations to bring your way. Again, it doesn't deal in specifics, but rather emotions and imagery. It doesn't know the difference between feeling happy to be alive or winning the lottery. If you think in a positive and grateful manner, you will simply bring yourself more to be grateful for.

I once knew a high level executive who used to valet his car outside of his favorite restaurant in California each week. However he could never understand why the parking attendant would always place his car two blocks away, instead of just across the road as he'd instructed. He would get so frustrated by having to wait an extra 5 minutes for his vehicle each time, it almost sent him into a frenzy. He would ask me what he should do about it, as he noticed I was much calmer in similar situations.

I simply asked him to think about it for a moment. What would he rather, be an important and well paid executive who had the opportunity to valet his top of the range Mercedes at his favorite restaurant every week. But have to wait an extra five minutes for it each time he left. Or be the guy who has to valet cars and survive off tips for a living? His outlook on the situation immediately changed. "You're right he replied, what was I thinking? I'll give the guy a break from now on".

Whilst I certainly do not like to waste my own time and believe in attaining efficiency whenever and wherever possible in life. I can

STOICISM

also notice the bigger picture and ensure I'm not "sweating the small stuff" to the detriment of my mindset. Being grateful for the things you do have has such a big impact in being able to achieve this.

I often quote a passage from *Meditations* by Marcus Aurelius, in which he states: "Do not indulge in dreams of what you don't have, but instead count the blessings you do possess, and then remember with thanks how you would desire them if they were not yours". In other words, we should constantly strive to be grateful for what we do have, instead of obsessing about what we do not.

Remember that in our modern world we enjoy a standard of living which even our grandparents would have found unimaginable. My executive friend certainly needed reminding of this. I'm not saying don't push for your loftier goals and a better life. Just temper this with an appreciation for what you do have in the here and now. Again, this isn't being thankful for the sake of it. It's another mind trick which propels us to greater success.

Most folks (myself included from time-to-time) fall into the trap of thinking that they will be happy at some future point in time, when they have achieved a certain level of attainment. Whether that be in their career, monetary terms, a relationship goal or status in general. This is again the wrong way of thinking. The mind doesn't know the difference between now and this future point. In reality, that future point will be "in the now" when it arrives anyway.

One way to put this into practice is to note down everything for which you are grateful for now. From the smallest observation to your biggest achievement. Then look at this list each morning when you wake, and before going sleep each night. Really feel what it's like to unconditionally appreciate these things and attach as much positive emotion to them as possible. You're subconscious is most in tune during these times and will go into hyper drive to serve up bigger and better things to be grateful for in lightening speed. Your creativity centers get switched on to the max, and you will notice that you are finding solutions to your problems with incredible ease.

CHAPTER 8: USE ROLE MODELS WISELY

If you ask anyone who's achieved any level of success in this world, whether that be in business, sport, raising a family and so on. They will almost certainly attribute a large part of their success to the mentors they followed. The shoulders of the giants they stood upon to get where they are today. Yes it took work on their part, persistent and massive action most likely. But they received a guiding hand to show them the path in the first place.

Mentors are great for this. They are usually up and close personal encounters. There is a proximity which makes the learning and feedback truly valuable. As I have previously mentioned, fulfilling ones purpose typically involves 'giving back' at some stage. This is why this mentor/student relationship is so prevalent and vital for human progression, as this knowledge and wisdom is passed down from one generation to the next.

However, there is a fine line between a mentor and a role model. The former can be interacted with, the latter must be appraised from afar. I'm not saying that roles models are inherently bad or misleading. But it takes a leap of faith and judgement call on our part regarding their true core values and intentions.

In today's world there is an abundance of role models we can follow. Celebrities, self-help gurus and business leaders all with their own YouTube channels spouting endless amounts of sometimes questionable content on a daily basis. Again, I'm not suggesting that this is entirely negative. Just to be aware of the downsides to the abundance of viewpoints.

First of all, there is the question of who do you actually listen to? Many of these people will have contradictory advice, although both holding merit of their own. I would suggest finding one or two roles models in your area of interest, then study everything they do and say. You will then get a deep enough insight into what made them as successful as they are. You will also get a slightly different perspective and angle on how to approach things yourself, but without to much confusion and contradiction.

Stop Idolizing

Once you have selected your "go to" role models, it's imperative to foster a healthy relationship with them. I say relationship, but that would require reciprocal interaction. It's more about how you absorb and integrate their content, message, knowledge and behaviors.

Yes its completely fine to look to others for inspiration, but never put someone on a pedestal just because they have achieved something you wish for yourself. These people have personality faults like everyone else, they are not perfect. Viewing them as such will elevate them to god status in your mind, and you will perceive their success to be out of reach for yourself.

As the Stoic forefathers continually point out. Life is to be lived by oneself. At some stage you will have to follow your own path. You are required to garner your own experiences and integrate these lessons into your psychological make-up, in order to ultimately become a more well rounded and resilient individual.

And finally, never give tacit approval to others. This can be especially common with people you respect and even view as mentors or role models. What do I mean by this? If somebody is explaining something to which we do not agree with, a common tendency is to simply nod ones head or say nothing at all. This indicates to the other person, and any by standers for that matter, that we agree with their position by default. Or we certainly do not disagree enough to pull them up on what they are saying.

Always be clear with your thoughts and morals at all times. Regularly question what others are espousing when around you. Words and clarity of thoughts matter, they form the basis of our arguments and our subsequent behaviors in the world. Never give tacit approval to questionable statements, especially if they run counter to your morals and virtues. You will respect yourself so much more when you do.

CHAPTER 9: DIE BEFORE YOU DIE

"Death is a stripping away of all that is not you. The secret of life is to "die before you die" and find that there is no death."

(Eckhart Tolle)

I previously stated my admiration for the work of Eckhart Tolle. Some view him as a new age, esoteric self-help guru. Others believe him to be an important spiritual sage capable of transforming the negative thinking patterns which plague the west. Remember, what is true for you, is ultimately true. But regardless of how you view Tolle's teachings on transcendence. Much of his advice on clearing the mind, differentiating between the observer and mindless chatter, can have profound effects on the person who chooses to implement this advice in their own lives.

Perhaps the most profound of these concepts is the notion of "dying before you die". I remember reading this for the first time being awestruck by the implications of this advice. It immediately resonated with my own thoughts on existence up until this point. It also struck a cord with much of the Stoic writings I'd been avidly consuming, no more so then within Seneca's "Letters From A Stoic".

If there was one Stoic forefather who understood the existential questions of the human experience more deeply then anyone else, it was Seneca. The following are just a few of his thoughts on the notion of life and death:

"You want to live, but do you know how to live? You are scared of dying and, tell me, is the kind of life you lead really any different from being dead?"

"He who fears death will never do anything worth of a man who is alive."

"This is our big mistake: to think we look forward to death. Most of death is already gone. Whatever time has passed is owned by death."

Most of us are far to caught up with our day-to-day activities to ever really contemplate these questions. We live as though set-backs and failure could kill us immediately, but waste time as if we will live forever. It's said that a person is no more alive then when they no longer fear death. It strips away all of the neuroses which get in the way of truly living. This applies to whatever you are trying to achieve, whether that be peace of mind or making millions of dollars. Really grasping this concept allows you to experience both, and anything and everything for that matter, all at the same time.

So few of us really go for it in life. We are neutered as toddlers to take the safe route. To be careful, avoid danger and stop causing havoc around the house. As babies we were ruthless in getting what we wanted. Screaming in the middle of the night for a bottle was no problem. Repeating the same meltdown just a few short hours later in order to get our diapers changed without a seconds thought.

It's a similar concept to taking massive and persistent action. We crawled all day long trying to reach our feet . There was never a thought of "oh, I fell down 3 times today, I'll give up on this walking business, it's too difficult". We continued on as if life wasn't worth living until we'd achieved it, and we were right. We were born race cars, but society soon turns us into milk trucks. We plod along as productive citizens never straying too far outside of our own lane. We were shaped perfectly to meet the needs of the industrial revolution factories, and now the office cubicles of the corporate world. If anything, our job is to return to that early state of ruthless action and risk taking behavior at breakneck speeds.

Once again, the advice here is not to be reckless. It's to continually look for problems to solve in order to grow. To expand your comfort zone and achieve so much success that any small amount of adversity will just be water off a ducks back. They won't even register as problems anymore. Recognizing that we are all in fact mortal beings with a physical shelf life here on this planet, frees us to follow our purpose unencumbered by the restrictions of fear. It affords us of the freedom and clarity of

JAMES DAUGHERTY

thought to develop our most creative nature. Don't be the person who played it safe just to ensure they reached the finish line in one piece. Don't always opt for the long iron to remain on the fairway. Dust off the driver and risk the rough. Die before you die, and be all you can be.

SUMMARY

"Everything can be taken from a man but one thing: the last of human freedoms. To choose ones attitude in any given set of circumstances, to choose ones own way"

(Viktor Frankl)

There is no getting away from the unfortunate fact that bad things happen to good people in life. Good employees lose their jobs, good business owners go out of business, good parents get sick children, good drivers get into bad accidents. If the teachings of stoicism has taught you anything at all, its this very fact. However, it is also one of the only mindset methodologies which attempts to address these instances head on. To ensure you can deal with these situations with courage and wisdom.

Viktor Frankl was an Austrian neurologist and psychiatrist who was also a holocaust survivor during World War II. Much of his psychological theories stem from his experiences within the Nazi concentration camps. During these times he would contemplate many existential questions. What is all this suffering for? What is life for? He quickly realized that it was he who had the choice to decide these things. It is us who can choose to feel apathetic and nihilistic towards life. If anybody had that right, it with

Frankl and the countless others who experienced these testing times.

However, Frankl chose the opposite. He chose to derive meaning from his life. He recognized that nobody could take this choice from him. They could take his freedom, liberties, clothing, food and pretty much every other basic human right. But they couldn't take away his ability to view the situation in the way he wished. Like many other concentration camp survivors, it was this which eventually got them through. It was identifying their purpose which kept them going.

You can read accounts of mothers staying in good spirits to eventually be re-connected with theirs sons and daughters, husbands to their wives and so on. If one is simply thinking of their own situation, regardless of how difficult it may be, we are much less powerless over it. This is why the opening chapter to this book relates to purpose over passion. I'm not suggesting that anyone who reads this is likely to face anything close to the stress of being a prisoner of war. But these extreme condition's serve to highlight a very important point.

On the face of things, these two concepts seem strikingly similar, inseparable to some perhaps. But there is a subtle yet distinct difference when we inspect them a little more closely. Purpose supersedes ones own wants, needs and desires. It requires

STOICISM

contribution to the greater good of humanity at large. Its the thing we were all put on this earth to find and strive for.

Passion on the other hand is individualistic, its a selfish notion by definition. Yes your passion may involve helping others, but I would argue that in fact you have probably found your true purpose if this is the case. I have no problem with people pursuing the things they enjoy doing. Spending leisure or downtime writing music, playing tennis or reading poetry. It's just a matter of where your focus lies. What do you want to spend the most creative and numerous hours in the day pursuing? What do you want to be remembered for when you are gone?

For most people, this will ultimately be pursing their purpose. Nothing gives you a sense of satisfaction and joy like being on the path to achieving your legacy. Laying your head on the pillow each night becomes far easier and more rewarding when you do so. That's not to say that unearthing this life mission will be easy. It will take much time and work to discover. This is where my next success principle comes in.

It will require persistent and massive action for the most part. This is where most people get self-help style mindsets and a law of attraction type mentality wrong. They believe that sitting in a dark room simply willing things into existence is the way to materialize them in their lives. This is only half of the battle. If you want to win the raffle, you have to buy a ticket! You can't sit around all day, you have to get moving.

Its about assessing your state and auditing your surroundings on a daily basis. If you are truly aligned with your purpose, this becomes much easier to do. Use thought pattern interrupts to snap yourself out of a funk. Re-read your goals and affirmations and make damn sure that you are in the company of those who promote similar values to your own. Maintaining this positive and productive mindset is critical to producing consistent and massive action. Plan for what you need to do, remove all distractions and become a dolphin.

A big part of this is doing what you say you will. A persons word seems to be worth much less in this day and age. Its one thing to be frivolous with commitments you make to other people, but its quite another when you do this with yourself. I now succeed in anything I do in life, not because I'm innately better than anyone else. I just trust myself to follow through on what I say I will do. I'm focused on bringing what I choose to bare into existence and not stopping until I do.

Much of this is down to not making any excuses for mistakes. If I were to do so it would rob me of the power over the situation and my ability to fix it. I appreciate that this is not easy for most, especially if you have been around those with a victim mentality for much of your life. We all learn from our environment growing

STOICISM

up, and can't choose our immediately family. But we can change our outlook on these instances, in spite of these early experiences.

This is simply done by re-contextualizing these situations. By taking a different view point on problems, set-backs and momentary failure. To stop viewing them as inherently bad. Refrain from adopting the societal viewpoint that they should be avoided. On the contrary, you should be running full force into the gunfire so to speak! These instances are the only means for growth. They are the only way we can learn to adjust our approach and move forward. Ultimately success lies on the opposite side of these hurdles. So don't run from them, embrace them.

One additional way to get ahead of the crowd when it comes to life planning and success, is to learn the art of proper goal setting. I say art, but in truth its both a science and an art. This is because it's split into two distinct phases when done correctly. The first stage being more scientific. These are the short term goals we all need to guide near term progress. They are the KPI metrics we require to ensure we are on track and heading in the right direction. They are a tool for getting ahead in the short term, but this is where there effectiveness ends.

Goal setting with regards to the larger, purpose driven goals in life, takes a different approach. It requires a different outlook, one which is more aligned with how the human mind works. More specifically, how the subconscious mind works, as its this which will ultimately materialize these desires for you. It requires frequent and emotionally attached images to be displayed in your mind.

This is not day dreaming, but rather visualizing your future self and surroundings. You can be specific in terms of what clothes you are wearing or what car you are driving. However, its the overall feeling and emotion which this mind movie provides which is the important thing. The body can't go where the mind hasn't already been. So explore these visions thoroughly, and they'll start showing up in your physical world far sooner than you may think.

Remember that you are likely to pivot a number of times on the way to realizing these aims as well. So a better approach is to maintain the picture of who you want to be, but open to exactly what path and vehicle will take you there. Don't forget to properly assess this progress when you are on the path to success too. Most folks make the mistake of constantly looking forward to see how far they must travel en route to these larger and loftier goals.

Whilst you should always be keeping them in mind, a far better strategy is to look back on how far you have come more often. This will provide you with a sense of achievement, serotonin release and boost of motivation to carry on going. These larger goals are continually evolving, becoming more grandiose whilst also rolling back on you. So the best thing you can do is not continually beat

STOICISM

yourself up for not arriving at the destination yet, but rather enjoy the journey, or should I say the process.

Two other concepts which can help with this peace of mind and patience on the road to high achievement, is learning how to delay gratification and foster a sense of gratitude towards your current situation. If you are able to shift your thinking away from merely the results you are getting in the here and now, it will allow you to do the proper work necessary to reap the bigger rewards later on down the line. Yes, set you short term targets, but know that they are simply there to feed the snowball as it rolls down the hill. Being genuinely grateful for the things you do have in your life in the mean time, will also add to this momentum.

In addition to this, use role models in your life wisely. Do not idolize these individuals and create an unhealthy relationship with them. These people are not flawless and perceiving their achievements as out of reach for yourself, is hugely self-sabotaging. It's far better to find a mentor who has your best interests at heart. Always lead with what you can offer, how can you add value to this persons life. If you can do that, what you will receive in return can often be a lifetime of priceless guidance.

And finally, discover the art of dying before you die. This is the ultimate way to live a free and fulfilling existence. It sounds like a dramatic statement on first read, but it really only serves to highlight the inherent truth of our mortality. It's nothing to be afraid of, its something to be embraced, regardless of your beliefs on the true nature of reality. If we are indeed omnipotent souls traversing infinity, then why not make the most of this human experience? If we are simply highly evolved mammals whose lights go out when our flesh and bones are no more, then the game plan is exactly the same. Live as abundantly as possible, as we might not get a second chance!

CONCLUSION

"I judge you unfortunate because you have never lived through misfortune. You have passed through life without an opponent— no one can ever know what you are capable of, not even you."

(Seneca)

My aim for this final installment in the Stoicism series was to help you avoid this fate. To help you realize your full potential. Yes dealing with adversity in the correct manner is half of the battle. But you need to be more proactive than this, especially in these modern times when change is occurring far faster then ever before. In this day and age you need a better approach. You require the tools to really get ahead, to fill your life with so much progress and success, that many of the problems you face will no longer register as issues anymore.

Most people get into trouble these days as they have too much time on their hands. The devil makes use of idle thumbs. This is why I am cautious about spending too much downtime or even pursuing my hobbies and passions. A far better strategy is to find your purpose and go for it every minute of the day. It really does all stem from there. You will find yourself tapping into energy and creativity reserves you never thought you had. All of the subsequent psychological tricks and tactics seem natural and far easier to implement at this point.

I also wanted to end this series on the most positive note possible. I'm well aware that much of the Stoic teachings can seem drab and uninspiring at times, although still essential and needed wisdom. I wanted to tease out the more practical elements of these quotes, principles and writings. To turn these teachings into actionable steps which can be put to work in your own life.

Hell is not a fiery place we go when we die. Its meeting the person we could have become. It's acknowledging what our full potential truly was, but realizing we only fulfilled half of it at best. This is the ultimate tragedy in life. It's not that we didn't win the race, its that we never even entered it. It wasn't that we didn't achieve all we set out to do, it's that we never really rolled the dice to give ourselves a fighting chance.

The safest place in the Colosseum is in the center of the arena, not sitting within the stands where you can't effect anything. You can make some noise and cheer on your favorite gladiator to glory, but you are set to win nothing. Far better is to have your feet on the gravel holding your sword and shield. To be on the field with your helmet and pads where you can get in the game. So make sure you do not sit on the sidelines of your life, and watch it pass you by. Get some skin in your own game. You are the only opponent which matters.

The psychological techniques I have laid out in this book and others, will hopefully help you to do just that. Do not simply read over them and nod your head in agreement with these concepts. If they resonate with you, then start putting them into practice straight away. I can assure you, it will be well worth the time and effort.

BONUS CHAPTERS

(From "Stoicism: An Ex-SPY's Guide - Volume 1")

I have included these chapters from the first installment of the Stoicism series, to give you a background insight into some of the core principles of this philosophy. Some insights into the history of its teachings. If you have not read that first edition yet, then I highly recommend you do. However, the following will give you a good overview.

CHAPTER 1: STOICISM – WHAT IS IT AND WHERE DID IT COME FROM?

"A Stoic is someone who transforms fear into prudence, pain into transformation, mistakes into initiation, and desire into undertaking"

(Nassim Taleb)

Stoicism in essence, is a simple philosophy which can help make you a happier and more positive person. Although its roots date back to Ancient Greece, it has since found a receptive audience in the 21st century. There are many today who actively strive to practice its tenets and have even organized themselves into online communities who are supporting each others efforts. Holding virtual events such as Stoic Week, which challenges participants to live as Stoics for seven days.

However the majority of people still do not fully understand just what Stoicism is. If you were to ask them what exactly they believe being a Stoic entails, they will say things like "the ability to hide emotion, even when you are in pain, or undergoing some other adverse or intense feeling." Although keeping emotions under control is an important attribute of a Stoic mentality, it is not the only thing which defines Stoicism.

What is Stoicism?

So what exactly does the principle of Stoicism encompass? It is a school of thought which was founded and developed around 301 BC by Zeno of Citium. Its name comes from the *stoa poikile* or painted porch, from which teachers lectured to students. Stoicism emerged following the death of Alexander the Great in 323 BC, which resulted in the breakup of his great empire, and a period of political turmoil in which multiple parties were competing for power.

Stoicism aided its followers in coping with the social uncertainty of this period, and thus, quickly gained many adherents who helped to develop its tenets by applying them to their everyday lives. There were three prominent thinkers during this period who are seen as essential in the development of Stoicisms basic tenets:

Marcus Aurelius (121 AD to 180 AD) ruled as Emperor of Rome from 161 AD to 180 AD. He was the author of the book *Meditations*, a private diary in which he chronicled his struggle to live up to Stoic ideals and principles during the most difficult days of his reign.

Epictetus (55 AD to 135 AD) was a former slave who became a teacher of philosophy after he was freed. His *Handbook* and four volumes of the *Discourses* are among the foundational texts of

Stoicism, and were compiled by a former student via his lectures after his death.

Seneca (4 BC to 65 AD) was a statesman who was a tutor and adviser to the Emperor Nero, but who also wrote extensively about Stoicism and philosophy. His most prominent works regarding Stoicism are in the form of letters which he wrote to his friends, and which are collected in books such as *Letters from a Stoic* and *On the Brevity of Life*.

An important thing to bear in mind is that only a very small percentage of what the original Stoic teachers wrote survives today and thus, much of what is taught as Stoicism is based on the interpretation of scholars, and other practitioners of these fragments. However, there is general agreement that the following represent the basic principles of Stoicism:

Virtue

Virtue is defined as behavior which displays high moral standards, which highlights the idea that Stoicism is a philosophy which is to be put into practice, rather than simply being appreciated intellectually as abstract concepts (the chapters in the latter part of this book will help you do this). Stoics believe there to be four core virtues:

- Wisdom. This is a virtue which can be difficult to define, but is generally understood as being the determining factor on how we should behave in general. How we should act and think in the right way by integrating experience and knowledge. For the Stoics, the most important type of wisdom is the considerations of moral thinking (being able to distinguish right from wrong) and practicality (being able to make the right choices in line with this).

- Justice. This virtue refers to our ability to treat others fairly and with even-handedness, but also with kindness.

- Courage. For Stoics, this virtue encourages a willingness to face and master ones fears. This is especially relevant with regards to personal development and life choices.

- Temperance. Better known as moderation, is the virtue which relates to being able to control ones desires.

To the Ancient Stoics, cultivating virtue was often viewed as the most important thing a person could do. When we live in accordance with virtue, we are not only living in harmony with other people, but also with our basic nature as rational creatures, and with nature as a whole. In practical terms, this means we can face both difficult people, and physical adversity with patience, level-headedness and good grace.

For Stoics, virtue provides us with the means to develop into our best selves. In fact, they believed the ultimate goal of human striving is to achieve *eudaimonia*, a Greek word which loosely translates into "happiness/well-being" or "human flourishing". For Stoics, this simply meant living in harmony with nature.

Emotions

One of the biggest misconceptions regarding Stoicism, which I have already mentioned, is that practitioners of the philosophy do not display emotion. However, Stoics actually believe the opposite. They posit that a person certainly should show emotion, however divide these feelings into "good" and "bad". Bad or negative emotions, such as fear and anger, are those which are based on faulty judgments, such as when we take external events too seriously.

On the other hand, healthy and positive emotions are the result of making wise judgments. According to the Stoics, there are three general categories of favorable emotions:

- Joy or delight, which takes pleasure in what is genuinely positive (such as great human achievement) rather than regards to more superficial things.

- Discretion or caution, which is directed towards the elements of life which are genuinely harmful to us, such as vice and folly.

- Willing what is truly good, such as wishing the best for others and ourselves, rather than longing for things which are beyond our control, such as indiscriminate wealth and other peoples perception of us.

For Ancient Stoics, the ultimate goal was not to be emotionally deprived, or to become a person with a heart of stone. But rather to cultivate self-love as well as a genuine concern for others, but always tempered by wisdom. For instance, we can display our love for others by practicing philanthropy.

Of course, there are certain involuntary emotional reactions which we experience in certain situations, such as being startled or embarrassed. However we should not allow these limbic system, reflex-like expressions to develop into full-blown emotional displays. Instead we should choose how to respond to the situation logically, and after sound consideration.

Nature and Humankind

As I have already mentioned, one of the major goals of practicing Stoicism was to live in agreement with nature. For Stoics, there were three aspects to this:

1. Our inner nature, which represents our capacity for reason.

2. The nature of society and how we interact with the rest of humankind.

3. The nature of the external environment around us.

STOICISM

Thus, Stoics encouraged us to see ourselves as part of nature and of a greater whole. By not understanding this concept I.e. that we are indeed an integral part of our environment, we fail to understand the impact which our activities have on it. Thus, the result is people feel free to destroy the environment for profit, as they do not understand the impact they are having. Ultimately what occurs in nature, will also eventually impact everyone of us in exactly the same way.

They also believed that our inner nature connects people to others around them. When we develop our moral character, we are living in accordance with the world around us, and in harmony with others. By contrast, people who are not in touch with their own true nature, are always in conflict with others, and as a result are alienated from these groups more readily.

Stoicism has influenced scores of prominent people throughout history, including kings and presidents. Thomas Jefferson was said to have kept a copy of the works of Seneca on his bedside table at all times. While George Washington reportedly put on a play about Cato, a Roman Senator who was one of the most prominent practitioners of Stoicism, in order to inspire his men during the winter they spent at Valley Forge.

If you are interested in practicing Stoicism, it is important to remember that it is not intended to be a solution to all of life's problems. Instead, it is a tool which we can use to become better human beings. The famous adage that you shouldn't be wishing for an easy life, but rather the strength to endure a difficult one, couldn't be more apparent here. Stoicism in general, is the perfect mental vehicle anyone can use to make this a practicality in their everyday lives.

CHAPTER 2: EXPECTATIONS AND DEMANDS – DEALING WITH MODERN DAY LIFE

"The essence of philosophy is that we should live, so that our happiness depends as little as possible on external causes"

(Epictetus)

One of the proposed reasons to why Stoicism is gaining popularity once again, is to view its resurgence in the context of an increasingly troubled world. A world whose current conditions share many parallels with the widespread disarray which followed the death of Alexander the Great. Many people are feeling uncertain about the world we live in and the many problems we face, and are searching for more efficient coping mechanisms

Stoicism provides us with the tools not only to develop inner tranquility, but also to build self-reliance, all whilst learning how to act with virtue in accordance with reason and logic.

For instance, it provides us a framework to deal with the various anxieties of modern life, simply by teaching us not to worry about factors which are beyond our control. If this sounds familiar to you, it is because you have probably heard of the Serenity prayer, which states "God, give me the serenity to accept what I cannot change, the courage to change the things I can, and the wisdom to discern the difference".

As Epictetus mentions within the *Enchiridion,* "Some things are up to us and some are not". He then asks what is to be done, before providing the answer: "To make the best of what is within our control, and to accept the rest as it happens naturally".

These lessons are ones which we have to keep in mind when we are confronted with the many problems which we face today. For instance, we may be experiencing economic anxiety as to whether or not we will be able to find a job, or to hold on to our current one. Although it is our natural inclination to worry, this is an unproductive feeling. Instead, we should learn to take a step back and look at the situation in a more objective light. This will enable us to decide what we CAN DO, and to weigh our options with grace and equanimity.

One everyday situation in which a Stoic viewpoint would be helpful, is that of a motor accident which was not our fault. Of course, our natural inclination would be to get angry and begin shouting towards the other party. However you have to take a step back and ask, "Would that help? Would it not be better if I simply stepped out of the car, calmly assessed the damage, and exchanged insurance information with the other driver?"

The Art of Acquiescence

Stoicism also urges us not to simply accept our fate, but rather learning to love what is occurring around us. As Epictetus puts it, "Don't seek for things to happen as you wish they would, but instead wish that they happen as they actually will – and then your life will go well". The term for this type of attitude is the "Art of Acquiescence" and it basically refers to making the best of a bad situation.

However it is also worth remembering that sometimes, what seems like a setback, may in the long run, actually be a benefit. For instance, in 2008 LA Lakers coach Phil Jackson had to undergo surgery to repair a hip injury which had been bothering him for a a number of years. During his recovery period, he was confined to a special chair near the players, and could no longer walk around the court side as he was so used to doing. Although Jackson was worried this may hinder his coaching, he found that being on the sidelines above the player's bench actually increased his authority, and he was able to assert himself without being overbearing as he was in the past.

Avoiding the Materialism Trap

Another important lesson we can learn, is to avoid placing too much value on material things. As Epictetus put it, "Wealth consists not of having many possessions, but in having few wants". Modern society has become increasingly materialistic, as easy access to credit cards and other forms of consumer credit encourages us to spend more and more on luxuries and other non-necessities, even if we don't have the money to pay for them now.

After all, we can just pay for them later down the line, and we don't even have to pay the full amount. Advertising and mass media further encourage a culture of materialism as we are constantly shown lavish lifestyles which we are encouraged to aspire to. When we are presented with a new shiny object (car, house, toy etc) it creates a dissonance in our mind, to the point of unhappiness with the lack of such possessions.

The only way to escape from the materialism trap, is simply to start distinguishing between our needs and our wants. We can easily meet our needs, but our wants can be unlimited. You need to break this "keeping up with the Jones" mentality to truly free your self from this negative mental spiral.

Marcus Aurelius, in his *Meditations*, states: "Do not indulge in dreams of what you don't have, but instead count the blessings you do possess, and then remember with thanks how you would desire them if they were not yours". In other words, we should constantly cultivate an attitude of gratitude for what we have, instead of obsessing about what we do not.

In our modern world we enjoy a standard of living which our grandparents, and even our parents would have found unimaginable.

I'm not suggesting you should rest on your laurels, or even feel bad about this fact. However most people would do well to remember this, and should be appreciative of the benefits afforded to their current situation, which were not available to others in the past.

Thus, we should follow Marcus Aurelius' advice and try to imagine what life would be like if we did not have the things we take for granted now. For instance, what if we were unable to live in a comfortable house, or did not have many of the creature comforts, such as a computer with Internet connection we are currently enjoying. Imagining not having these things helps us to appreciate them more, so we are not always longing for the things that we do not have.

Learning How to Be Kind

Another modern issue which the Stoics seemed to have predicted is globalization. With advances in transportation and communication, the world seems smaller than it was in the past. We can now communicate with someone on the other side of the world in minutes or even seconds, and travel to far-flung destinations in a matter of hours. But recent trends towards nationalism seems to be making nations turn inward rather than building ties with other countries to create a truly global community.

According to Epictetus in his *Discourses,* when you are asked the question of what country you are from, do not say that you are from

Athens or Corinth, but rather that you are a "citizen of the world". It is our alienation from one another, as well as from nature, which has been the root of many of the modern problems we are facing. These include climate change, widespread income inequality and regional displacement of societies due to global conflict.

We can apply this attitude on the micro level as well, by attempting to be kinder to the people around us, even if they are strangers or mere acquaintances. As Marcus Aurelius put it, "Injustice often lies not just in what you are doing, but in what you are not doing". Inaction is often as bad as actively doing something harmful. So if we can perform acts of simple kindness, even for people we don't know, we are helping to promote justice in the world in our own small way.

Printed in the USA
CPSIA information can be obtained
at www.ICGtesting.com
LVHW011410051023
760085LV00065B/2518